*How You
See Anything
Is How You
See Everything*

# How You
# See Anything
# Is How You
# See Everything

*A Treasury of Simple Wisdom*

**Gail Van Kleeck**

**Illustrations by Lesley Avery Gould**

**Andrews McMeel
Publishing**

Kansas City

00 01 02 03 RDC 10 9 8 7 6 5 4 3 2

www.andrewsmcmeel.com

Library of Congress Cataloging-in-Publication Data

Van Kleeck, Gail.
How you see anything is how you see everything : a treasury of simple wisdom / words by Gail Van Kleeck ; drawings by Lesley Avery Gould.
    p.   cm.
ISBN 0-7407-0053-7 (hardcover)
1. Conduct of life.   I. Gould, Lesley Avery.   II. Title.
BF637.C5V36   1999
813'.54—dc21                                              99-18924
                                                              CIP

——————— ATTENTION: SCHOOLS AND BUSINESSES ———————

Andrews McMeel books are available at quantity discounts with bulk purchase for educational, business, or sales promotional use. For information, please write to: Special Sales Department, Andrews McMeel Publishing, 4520 Main Street, Kansas City, Missouri 64111.

*This book is tenderly dedicated to our mother,
who continually encouraged and supported our creativity,
and to our father, who illustrated by his life that integrity
and persistence always win.*

*Gail Van Kleeck*
*Lesley Avery Gould*

# Contents

# Acknowledgments

*How does anyone truly thank the people who have helped to carry her dream?*

*To my precious sister Lesley, my gratitude for naming this book and for creating the drawings that gave it life. To the incredible Debbie Yeoh, my endless thankfulness for the times she read and reread my words, then challenged me, with both her clarity and her wisdom, to be all that I could be. To Parker, my sweetheart, my tender appreciation for supporting me in following my muse, even when it took me away from him; and to my children and grandchildren, my abiding thanksgiving for their life-changing presence, which inspired me to persist.*

*I also wish to thank Arielle Eckstut, my agent, who believed in me and helped me to tell a more complete story, and Chris Schillig, my publishing editor, who caught the spark of my words and helped fan them into a fire.*

*And what would I have done without the encouragement of my family and the example of Carole and Connie and Gail and Joan and all of my many other friends, in whose wisdom and beauty and strength, I have come to discover my own?*

*My last and most important wish is to thank our Creator, who is the true author of this book.*

## Writer's Note

*When I asked my sister Lesley to illustrate this book, her own marvelous storytelling ability became apparent. Lesley tells with drawings the same sort of story I tell with words. For her, the little dog represents the endless presence of possibility while the figure represents the humanness in each of us as we struggle with, learn from, play with, and occasionally accept the rope of life, with all its ups and downs.*

*The story told by Lesley's drawings is not intended to
directly illustrate any of my words. Rather it overlays
another dimension, for how we see anything is always a
choice and it is in seeing that choice that we empower
ourselves to become all we were created to be.*

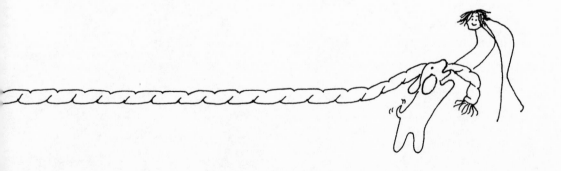

# Half of Eight

The colorfully dressed second-grade teacher stood with her back to the board, looking out at her class. She tucked a lock of partially graying hair behind her ear and smiled. Teaching for her was an experience of the heart. She had never stopped marveling at the children's sense of wonder and their excitement in learning.

"You're doing so well at addition and subtraction," she said encouragingly. "And now that you know your times tables, multiplying is getting easier too." She smiled again, focusing her energy on the children, who were still struggling with the concept, hoping to somehow reassure them. "Today we begin learning to divide. This is going to be fun, because you already know some of the answers." She paused for a moment, enjoying their sense of anticipation. "Who can tell me," she asked, "what number is half of eight?"

The classroom was suddenly filled with an ocean of

waving hands. "Half of eight is four," they called out excitedly. The teacher nodded. Sweeping her gaze across the room, she noticed that the tall, pale boy in the back row seemed uncomfortably silent.

The boy had arrived at the school late in the year, after many of the children's friendships had already been formed. While her instincts told her the child was intelligent, his shyness and lapses into a world of his own made him more difficult to reach. Now she could see he was puzzled by the class's response. Not wishing to add to his discomfort, she simply fell silent. "I don't understand," the boy said, almost to himself. "How can half of eight be four?"

A girl in the front row giggled. The teacher frowned her into silence. The tall, pale boy shuffled his feet and looked down at his hands. "Could I go show you something?" he asked shyly. "Of course," his teacher replied. Without

waiting for further encouragement, he walked slowly toward her and stood awkwardly in front of the class.

The teacher's heart felt heavy. Years of experience had taught her how often children need to find their own answers, but she was concerned about this lonely boy. She watched anxiously as he stepped to the board, took the chalk in his hand, and drew a large figure eight. For a moment he simply stood there; then, covering the top loop of the eight with his hand, he stepped back so his classmates could look. "See," he said shyly. "Half of eight is zero." Moving back to the figure on the board, he covered the left side with both hands. "Now," he explained, "half of eight is three."

Tears of understanding gathered in the teacher's eyes. Standing beside the boy, she placed her hands gently on his shoulders and turned him, so he could see both her and his classmates. "What a wonderful mind you have." The admiration in her voice was clear. "I've been teaching for a very long time, and no one has ever seen that possibility before! I can't wait to tell your parents and the other teachers what you've helped us discover today." The boy's thin shoulders straightened as he heard the murmurs of approval from his classmates.

"Now, let me show you something else." Pressing her thumbs into her palms, she held her hands toward him. "How many fingers am I holding up?"

"You are holding up eight fingers, four on each hand," the boy replied.

"Tell me what happens if I take half of them away," she asked, putting her right hand behind her back.

A smile lit the lonely boy's face. "You have four. I see now," he said, pleased by his own understanding. "Half of eight can also be four."

*Imagine*
*how our lives*
*might change*
*if we looked*
*through the eyes*
*of possibility.*

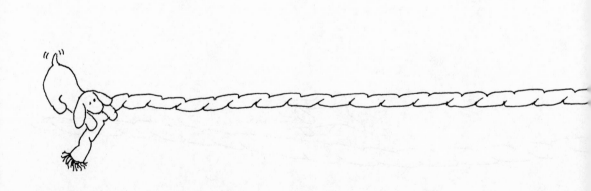

# The Little Bird

The young woman who knelt in her garden breathed in the cool fragrance of moist soil beneath her hands. After a long, cold New England winter, she felt especially grateful for the early spring day and the warmth of sun on her shoulders. Sitting back on her heels, she paused to watch her two small children as they entertained themselves nearby. Motherhood had changed her life in many ways, filling her with a tender sort of protectiveness that somehow always brought a lump to her throat.

Turning back to her garden, she reached around a low-growing bush to draw aside a pile of wet, brown leaves. At first she sensed rather than saw a movement. Looking more closely, she drew in her breath. Crouched at the base of the bush was a tiny, nearly featherless baby bird. Reaching out, she slid her fingers gently under the fragile creature's body and, calling the children to join her, carried him into the house.

The three of them fashioned a nest from a shoe box and propped the baby bird in a pile of soft cloth. "He's very weak," the mother said, hoping to prepare her children for what seemed almost inevitable. But, ignoring her concern, they rushed back outdoors, intent on digging worms. By the time they made their dirty but triumphant reappearance, the woman had already begun feeding the baby bird from a dropper filled with warm broth.

Throughout the night the woman woke herself for

feedings, much as she'd once awoken to feed her own children. By morning the tiny creature not only was alive but seemed somehow stronger. Heartened, they added baby food to his diet and began ringing a bell when they fed him, hoping he'd associate the sound with eating and come back to them after he was free. The little bird grew to love the sound of the bell, chirping so loudly each time it rang that the family named him Peep.

On warm days as he grew stronger, the three of them carried the little bird out onto the grass. To their amazement, his parents seemed to recognize him, flying to greet him with noisy exuberant chirps. But the children's mother, who had grown to love the tiny creature, had also grown afraid for him. She had visions of dogs and cats and other terrors.

Not trusting Peep's parents to care for him as well as she, she scooped him up and carried him back into the house.

Before long it became clear that Peep was teaching himself to fly. At first he simply fluttered furtively up onto the dog's awaiting back, but when he began soaring proudly and unerringly onto both furniture and shoulders, the family knew in their hearts that the time had come to set him free.

On the morning of his "freedom day" they held a farewell ceremony in the front yard, then watched as Peep fluttered toward a low branch. Each afternoon after that, concerned that he hadn't yet learned to find his own food, the mother rang his feeding bell.

The early spring weather turned suddenly cold, and she drew on her sweater before stepping outdoors. This time as

Peep swooped joyfully toward her, he failed to see the badminton net the family had stretched in the front yard just the night before. Flying into it, the little creature tore his fragile wing and crashed headlong to the ground.

Rushing to her beloved bird, the distraught mother cradled him gently on her lap as she drove to the vet. Shaking his head, the kindly man pressed a vial of chloroform into the woman's unwilling hand.

Back at home, she placed Peep in his little shoe box and laid the opened vial beside him. Whispering their good-byes, she and the children stroked his soft, gray feathers one last time and reluctantly drew the lid into place. Long after the faint fluttering within the shoe box had ended, the mother's hands still trembled.

Other springs have come since then. Peep's parents seem to bear the family no ill will. They have blessed them with other nests and countless babies. Yet often when the children's mother finds herself thinking she knows what is best for someone else, she remembers Peep, and how great a price he paid so she might learn a lesson.

When we try too hard
to protect those we love,
our fears may
actually keep them
from joys
and possibilities
we cannot know or see.

# The Misty Morning

The little girl drew on her shorts and shirt, then, pausing for one last look at her sleeping family, tiptoed out the door. The early-morning world was filled with quiet calls of waking birds. A small striped chipmunk crossed the old dirt road ahead of her and, glancing curiously at this youthful human intruder, hurried on his way. Following the winding road toward the lake, the child resisted her urge to run the last few yards and stood perfectly still for a moment, as though to breathe in the view.

The flat, silver surface of the water was shrouded in an early-morning mist. It reminded her of the magic lands in her book of fairy tales. Smiling happily, she ran down the slight incline toward her beloved boat.

The old aluminum craft was tied securely to a tall white birch. The girl slipped the weathered oars into their oarlocks and pulled on a faded orange life jacket that was waiting for her there. Drawing a deep breath of satisfaction, she waded out into the water to push the boat away from shore.

Her father had taught her to row when she was only five. She had sat on the seat between his legs while both of them held the oars. On her sixth birthday he had moved to another seat, so she could row without him. Now that she was seven, although the boat belonged to her family during the day, in these magic morning hours it was hers alone.

Arching her back, the girl pulled against the water, moving the boat slowly forward. She watched as droplets gathered on the tips of her oars, then dripped silently back into the lake.

The oars cut smoothly into the water again, as she practiced her best Indian technique so as not to make a splashing sound. Farther down the beach a blue heron, who stood knee-deep in the water, watched patiently as a sparkling school of minnows swam closer to his legs. The girl smiled, then, lifting one oar, pulled hard against the other and pointed her boat in the opposite direction.

A giant dragonfly, with wings as translucent as deep green glass, drifted down and perched beside her as she rowed. In the distance she heard the splashing of a fish, then noticed that the mist had slipped away.

"Breakfast must be nearly ready," the girl thought

hungrily, heading her craft toward the shore. When she felt the gentle grating of sand beneath the bow, she sprang easily over the side and dragged the old boat back to its place beneath the tall white birch.

Slipping out of the life jacket, she paused to look at the scene, then laughed aloud. "I can't imagine a better morning," she thought. "I loved being out there on the water all by myself. I wonder what it will be like when I get older and Daddy lets me untie the boat from this tree." She coiled the long, wet rope that had connected her craft to the shore throughout her morning's adventure and hurried home to breakfast.

*Perhaps the secret*
*of happiness*
*lies in seeing*
*the wonder of life*
*even within the boundary*
*of our limitations.*

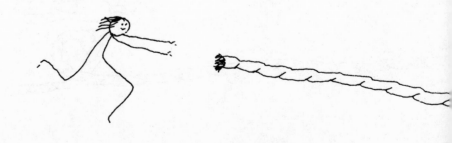

# Making Stroganoff

"That's it, I've had it! This is the very last straw!" The "thirty-something" suburban housewife brushed the long, red hair from her face and angrily pushed her chair back from the kitchen table. Striding to the window, she stood silently, staring out past the glass without really seeing, then lowered her eyes to reread her mother-in-law's letter.

"My Dear:" The words spread themselves before her through a thick, hot blur of tears. "I've enclosed a list of the words you misspelled in your last note to me. I hope your children don't inherit that trait from you. While it was good to have the four of you with us, I do wish our son would come by himself next time. You and the children cause more confusion than we like, and your father-in-law has come down with a cold, which he probably caught from somebody's runny nose. I've practically made myself sick too, thinking about what I'll serve at the bridge club on Friday. I hope the migraine you had when you were here is better and that you'll talk to our son about visiting us alone. Love, Mother."

"Love!" thought the young wife, crumpling the letter in her hand. "She doesn't know the meaning of the word!

"How many years?" she wondered, seeing the garden beyond her window for the first time. "How many years have I tried everything I know to earn her approval and acceptance? Nothing I do counts for anything. In the end, it's always the same. I feel so resentful, sometimes I think I hate her!" The anger she suddenly felt shocked the young woman. "I need to do something to get my mind off all this." Turning, she dropped the letter in the wastebasket and opened the refrigerator door.

While she had never thought of herself as a gourmet cook, there were a few things the woman made reasonably well. One of them was Stroganoff. Through years of experimentation she'd found just the right combination of wine, mushrooms, and lots of sweet yellow onions. Her family loved the dish, and she'd bought the meat to make it just the day before. Now she cut off the fat, dredged the beef in seasoned flour, and began browning it lightly.

For a moment the woman forgot about her mother-in-law's letter, thinking instead of the dinner she and her family would be sharing that night. She smiled at the thought of using their good dishes, picking a bouquet of wildflowers,

and remembering to light the candles. "We save candlelight for special moments," she mused. "Sometimes we forget every moment is special."

Reaching into the drawer where she kept the onions, she was completely taken aback to discover it was empty. "It's all right," she reassured herself, picking up the phone. "I'll just borrow some from my neighbor." But the neighbor had just used her last onion in a stew.

The young woman rinsed her hands, took the meat from the pan and reached for the car keys.

"Well, this is just perfect," she thought sarcastically, turning her vehicle into the grocery store's parking lot and searching frantically for a space. "As hard as I try to be a good daughter-in-law, that self-centered old woman still refuses to give me the acceptance and approval I need. Now, even though I've been a good neighbor, I still have to go out and get my own onions. Life just isn't fair!

"There'll be no time now for setting out the good dishes and picking a bouquet of wildflowers," she thought, walking wearily back into her kitchen. "Well, at least we can have candlelight." She reached for her favorite candlesticks, hoping somehow to make herself feel better.

As she set the table for dinner, she thought about her day. While she'd been disappointed when her neighbor couldn't give her onions, the woman realized she had felt neither anger nor resentment toward her. "She didn't intend to make my life difficult," she thought. "She just couldn't give me something she didn't have."

Her mind drifted back to her mother-in-law's letter and to the years she'd spent trying to earn the older woman's

acceptance and approval. "Maybe acceptance and approval just aren't part of her nature." It was a new and somewhat startling thought. She shook her head sadly. "Maybe she's not withholding anything from me after all. Maybe she simply can't give me something she doesn't have."

She sighed. Although she was still feeling disappointed, she noticed that some of her anger had been replaced with understanding. She stared silently into the light of the candles she'd just lit, then, dishing up the Stroganoff, carried it quietly to the table.

*Sometimes we need
to take a second look
at our expectations.
How foolish it would be
to be angry at a beggar
for not giving
us pearls.*

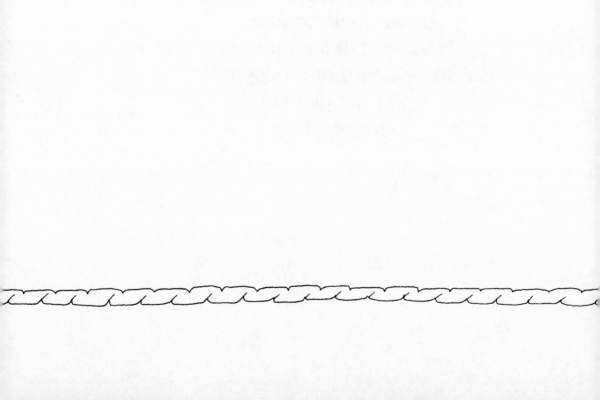

# Hasten Slowly

"Aren't you a little old to begin a project like this?" the man's son-in-law asked, looking up from the blueprint.

The older man nodded. "Maybe," he said, understanding. "Guess that just means I'd better not waste any time getting started." He lifted the drawings from the table and carried them out to the huge, flat platform he'd already built behind the toolshed in his yard.

It was early spring, and the bare, black branches of the old oak tree stood still and silent as he worked. Following a number-filled diagram, he divided the platform into grids, then drove strategically placed nails halfway down into the wood. The new-green leaves on the tree were quietly unfolding by the time he had finished.

"Doesn't look very impressive," his son-in-law teased,

glancing at the platform and picking up the blueprint to study it more closely. The man was too busy to listen. Carefully bending long, thin strips of wood around the nails, he marked their curves with a red drawing pen, then, pleased with his progress, transferred the marks to a paper pattern.

Setting up his table saw beneath the leafy, dark green shadow of the old oak, the man transferred the patterns onto the strong, wide boards he'd so painstakingly bolted together. By the time this part of his task was complete, a carpet of red and gold leaves covered the ground at his feet.

"It still doesn't look like much," his son-in-law said, surveying the bolted boards and the frame that stood like a

backbone between them. The older man ran his hand fondly across one of the curved pine planks and smiled. He was already designing a covering for his project and was too pleasantly preoccupied to talk.

As the first snowflakes drifted softly to the ground, the man completed his greenhouselike enclosure and moved the saw inside. All through the winter he measured, bolted, leveled, and glued. By the time his son-in-law returned, the snow had melted and the naked black branches of the oak were once again waiting impatiently for spring. "At this rate, it will take you years to finish," the younger man said, silently surveying the structure.

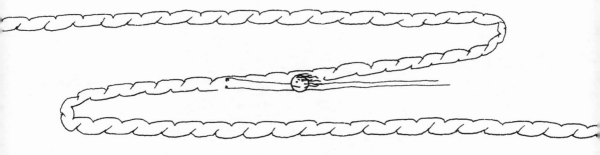

"Life isn't just about completion," his father-in-law replied, glancing up from the nail he was driving.

"When you look at all of this," he said, waving his hand in the direction of the structure, "you see the impractical project of an old man and the almost hopeless endlessness of my task. When I look at it, I see the curve of the wood and the shape of the dream I've carried all my life.

"I don't spend much time thinking about how long it will take me to finish this boat." He paused to stroke one of the thin mahogany planks he'd begun laying onto her hull. "What I see, is how far I've already come."

*What we see*
*in life*
*often depends*
*on what*
*we're looking for.*

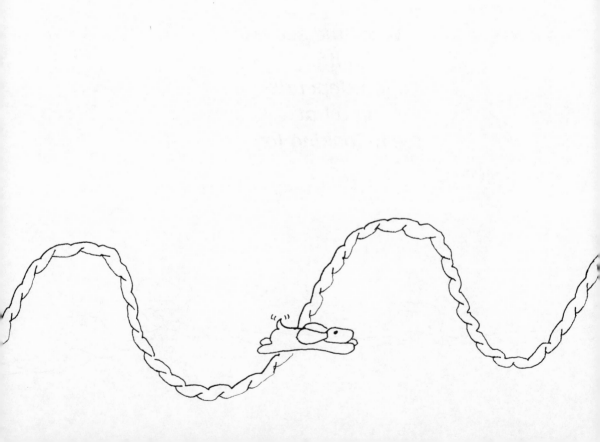

# Just Like You

The grandmother closed the storybook and laid it quietly aside. "You were asleep long before I finished," she said, smiling at the little child. "Your daddy used to do that too." The night-light touched her granddaughter's face, casting gentle shadows on the wall. "When he and your auntie were children," she went on, "he was the busiest one. She loved music and quiet games, but your daddy was a more challenging child. He was on the go from the moment he woke up till the time we tucked him into bed. Sometimes at the end of an especially exhausting day, I'd slip into his

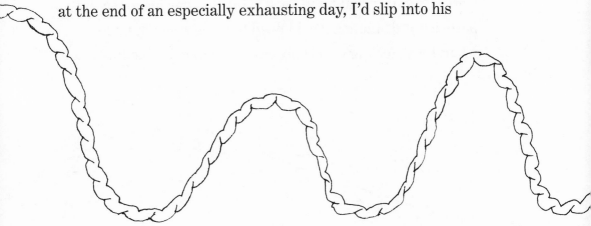

room, just to watch him sleep. 'I hope all your children are just like you,' I'd whisper wearily, then tiptoe off to bed.

"You wouldn't believe all the trips we made to the emergency room," she confided to her sleeping granddaughter. "He moved so quickly, he was always getting hurt. Sometimes when we were rushing to the hospital, I'd tell him how much I hoped all his children would be just like him. I suppose I wanted him to know how it felt to be the parent of such an active child.

"Almost from the beginning, your daddy pushed against every boundary and limit we set. I had never imagined my patience and stamina would need to stretch so far. Once, when I was feeling especially tired, I remember yelling after him as he went out to play, 'I hope all your children are just like you!'

"After a while he grew up and fell in love with your mommy, then before very long you were born." The grandmother sat quietly for a moment, looking at the miracle of the sleeping child.

"You are the most beautiful and precious of all God's gifts," she thought lovingly. "You're wise and tender and loving and smart . . . and a handful too," she acknowledged, smiling to herself. For a moment, in the dim glow of the night-light, the woman glimpsed the childhood face of her sleeping son, and a feeling of remorse, so strong it made her ache, silently slipped itself across her heart.

"All those times he was loving and tender and wise and smart," she thought, feeling suddenly ashamed, "I never once told him I hoped his children would be just like him. I never used those words to show how much I loved him, how grateful I felt to be his mother, and what an indescribable blessing he was in my life."

In the silence of the darkened room, the grandmother bowed her head and wept, touched by the unnameable sorrow of the words she'd left unsaid.

"The truth is," she thought, wiping her eyes and looking again at her granddaughter, "I got my wish." She bent to straighten the child's blanket, then tiptoed silently from the room "She's exactly like her father," she said, smiling. "I can't imagine a finer thing to be!"

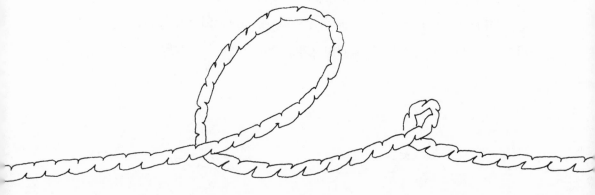

*When we speak*
*only part of the truth,*
*it can often become*
*the only part*
*we see.*

# The Dance

She'd turned thirty-eight just three days before she signed up for the class in personal communication. She had two children, a husband, a home, and a fledgling business. She also had responsibilities to her parents, her siblings, her friends, and the PTA. It wasn't as though she was looking to add one more thing to her life. She was already so busy she scarcely had time for herself, but her friend was beginning a teaching career, and she wanted to support her endeavor.

There were fifteen other women in the room that first day. Though they came in different shapes and sizes, their

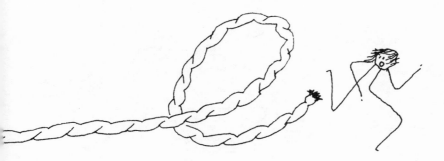

lives were in many ways like hers. Her friend asked everyone to get a notebook for keeping a journal. Some of the women groaned, but the woman who'd just turned thirty-eight was pleased. She liked writing. The class was beginning to look as though it might be fun. "One more thing," the instructor interjected. "This journal is just about you, so don't write about anyone else."

Early the next morning the woman settled herself at the desk. Anxious to begin, she opened the new notebook and rested the tip of her pen on its first page. The pen didn't move. She simply couldn't write about herself without including someone else. For the first time in longer

than she could remember, she laid her head on her arms and sobbed.

It wasn't as though she resented any of her roles or relationships. She had willingly and happily added all of them to her life. She felt proud of her accomplishments and glad for the opportunity to care for others. But more and more she felt caught in a dance of demanding, swirling partners, with no time to rest, no choice in the music, and no opportunity to dance alone. As the tempo increased, the woman saw herself moving faster and faster until she disappeared, dissolving into the other dancers through the gray-blue mist of her tears.

Days passed, then turned slowly into weeks. At first the woman sat at her desk every morning, hoping something would change. "I've lost myself completely," she thought miserably, feeling the depression set in.

It had been more than a month since she'd attempted to write. Her depression had deepened until it seemed to color everything in her life. Sitting despondently at the desk, she stared unseeing at the bleak whiteness of her paper, then, guided by something deep within her, reached hesitantly for the pen. "Dear Friend," she wrote. "This letter is to introduce myself to you."

The words and feelings that had eluded her for so long ran eagerly toward her, until she could scarcely write fast enough to capture them.

The woman wrote about her childhood and her painfully shy teenage years. "Motherhood," she said, "was the most heartwrenchingly beautiful experience of her life." There were no words deep enough, wide enough, or full enough to express the love and devotion she felt toward her children. She spoke with bittersweet longing about the loneliness of her marriage and of the ever-increasing times she felt responsible and guilty for falling short of being the kind of wife, mother, or person she thought she should be.

She relived long, gentle summer days at an old farm in Maine, walks in the country, evenings filled with stars. She smiled at the thought of how much she still loved the smell of puppy's breath and fresh sheets on a line.

"More than anything," she said, "she wanted to make a

difference in the world." There was a book she dreamed of writing, but there was too much else to do. There was no time for that sort of dreaming. Instead she felt increasingly exhausted and overwhelmed by her responsibilities, and so achingly hungry for acknowledgment and understanding that sometimes in the deepest, darkest part of her spirit she wondered if it would be easier to be dead.

The woman rubbed her cramped fingers. "This could take a lifetime to write," she thought, quietly teasing herself, "but it's a good start." She carried the letter with her to a chair by the window, sitting to reread it as though it had come from a friend.

As she read, she sometimes forgot she was the letter's

author, appreciating instead the woman's humor, goodwill, and gentle honesty. She was filled with a deep sense of tenderness and compassion for this clearly caring person who seemed to ask so much of herself and so little from life.

"I never understood till now," she thought, placing the letter on her lap and gazing through the window. "How could I have hoped to respect and respond to the needs of others when I haven't acknowledged or honored my own? If I were to write a few pages of this letter every day," she mused, "perhaps I might get to know myself well enough to write that book I've been dreaming about."

Walking slowly to the stereo cabinet, she searched

through her collection for the exact song she had in mind. "Maybe I can choose the music for this dance after all."

She gazed in recognition at the face looking back at her through the front hall mirror. "Hello," she said, holding out her hand in friendship. "It's nice to know you. May I have the pleasure of this dance?"

*As we begin
to see ourselves
more clearly,
the dance of life
becomes more honest,
healing,
and hopeful.*

# The Horses That Throw Us

The man who sat behind the long mahogany executive desk shrugged his shoulders up as far as they would go, then allowed them to drop, hoping to relieve the knot that was tightening in his neck. While he was sure no one knew the ins and outs of the business world as well as he, lately the fun had gone out of it. He was weary of the politics and confrontation. Nothing in his life seemed to be working. His wife had moved with their daughter to a small apartment in the next town, and the disagreements with his staff were growing more heated and frequent.

The framed photo of a huge Clydesdale hanging on the wall opposite his desk caught the man's eye. These horses,

he knew, had been bred to carry King Arthur's fully armored knights. Riding such an animal had been his boyhood dream.

For a brief moment he smiled, remembering the evening the Clydesdale named Ulysses had been delivered to the enclosure behind his home. He could still hear the stomping and smell the aroma of fresh manure emanating from the van. Although the yearling colt weighed nearly a ton, his endearing clumsiness had quickly earned him the nickname Baby Hewie.

It was getting late. The man gathered up his papers, stuffed them into a briefcase, and left the office.

While he had no experience in horse training, he had worked with Hewie nearly every night since his arrival, piling heavy grain bags on the horse's back and speaking reassuringly as the animal circled him from the end of a long rope tether. Over time the man had grown so comfortable with Hewie's patience and friendly responsiveness that he felt both confident and self-assured.

So it was, on that evening in early spring the man donned his work boots and an old motorcycle helmet. Carrying the kitchen stool out into the paddock, he stood on tiptoe and spoke in low, comfortable tones while easing an old saddle onto Hewie's high, broad back.

The horse, who stood patiently, flinched a little as he felt the girth strap tighten, but the saddle was lighter than his work harness, and in a moment he was quiet. Climbing cautiously up onto the stool, the man eased himself gently into the saddle. Hewie didn't move.

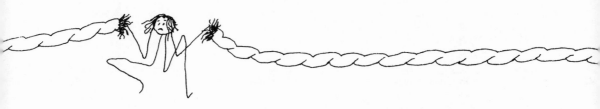

Holding the reins in one hand and stroking the animal's muscular neck with the other, Hewie's owner smiled. He thought briefly that warnings about partially broken horses and inexperienced riders didn't apply if the two had established a bond of friendship and trust. It was a magnificent moment.

The next moment was not so magnificent. Hewie had taken a few seconds to assess the situation. While a person on his back was no heavier than grain bags, something seemed different. Eyes white-rimmed, nostrils flaring, the horse's body convulsed in a frenzy of rearing, bucking terror, which propelled his would-be rider in an agonizingly long arc across the still frozen paddock.

Although bruised and badly shaken, the man remembered the old adage about getting back on the horses that throw us. Readjusting the motorcycle helmet and fighting to ignore his trembling legs, he once again carried the kitchen stool to Hewie's enormous heaving side. This time the horse was ready for him. Before his rider was fully in the saddle the ton of terrified animal reared. Pawing the air with platter-size hooves, he threw the frightened man off to the side, coming down only inches from his head.

Hewie's fallen owner summoned his strength and crawled painfully to the edge of the paddock. Using the fence post for support, he dragged himself into an upright position. "Maybe riding Hewie is a little like living life," he thought ruefully. "While we need to get back on the horses that throw us, we need to be willing to change something first."

Hewie moved slowly toward his owner, nuzzling him tentatively as though to reassure them both. "I want us to

ride peacefully together, fella," the man said gently, feeling the horse's warm breath on his neck. "There are so many wonderful places to go." He fell silent for a moment as the beginning of an idea took shape in his mind.

"You're not afraid of the weight on your back," he said, stroking the horse absently. "I'm not nearly as heavy as the grain bags. Maybe you were frightened by the touch of my legs. What if I changed the bags, so they hung down on both sides? Maybe if we practiced that till you got more comfortable, the ride would be better for both of us."

Battered, weary, and yet hopeful, Hewie's owner limped slowly back to his house. "Maybe grain bags aren't the only things in my life that need changing," he thought. Reaching for the telephone, the man dialed his wife's number.

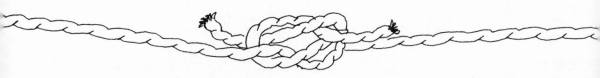

*Perhaps nothing*
*in life*
*can really change*
*until we look*
*for the changes*
*we can make*
*in ourselves.*

# Silver Skates

The lanky, redheaded boy parked his car in front of the familiar gray cottage. Bounding up the steps two at a time, he let himself in. His grandmother's home was rarely locked. Smelling faintly of wood fires, vanilla-scented candles, and garlic, it greeted him, as did she, with the comfortable feeling of acceptance he'd learned to anticipate and rely on.

"We're all packed," he said, returning her hug. "My friend and I leave tomorrow. We're going to take the whole month to drive cross-country before we start college. It's going to feel like a completely new life." He hesitated a moment. "I brought my itinerary notebook to show you. We've spent a long time working out all the details."

"I'd love to look at it." His grandmother smiled. "It will

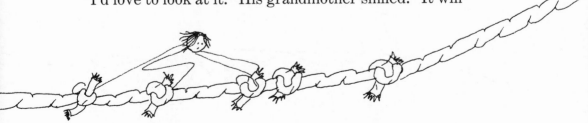

make me feel as though I'm going with you." The boy drew in his breath as though he was packing the memory of all this to take with him on his journey.

She wasn't the "milk and cookies" sort of grandmother he'd once wished she would be. She loved to sing, liked off-color jokes, celebrated the outrageous, and loved him absolutely, without condition or judgment. She was often stubborn, sometimes wise, occasionally funny, and consistently able to see the possibilities in life. He was going to miss her.

They walked together to the picnic table in her garden and spread the loose-leaf notebook out between them. The boy and his friend had charted every day so completely that by the time they reached the final page his grandmother felt as weary as though she had made the trip herself.

"You've certainly been thorough," she exclaimed, closing the book gently and looking at the boy.

"We didn't want to leave anything out," he said proudly. "We wanted this trip to be everything we expect it to be."

His grandmother nodded. "I remember feeling like that once too," she said, smiling. "I was about nine years old at the time, and my friends and I decided to have an unbirthday party."

"What's that?" asked her grandson.

"It's a party where nobody has a birthday and everyone gets a present," replied his grandmother, with a smile of remembering in her eyes. "We all drew names for the gift giving. No one was supposed to know whose name we drew or what the present would be."

"That sounds like fun."

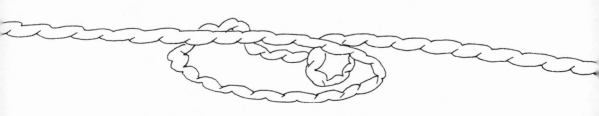

"It was," answered the grandmother, patting his hand.

"When I looked at my paper, I realized I'd drawn my best friend's name, and I could tell she'd drawn mine too. It was very exciting. We decided to have a special secret. We decided to go shopping together, so each of us could choose exactly the present we wanted."

"It sounds like a good idea," said her grandson, hardly able to imagine his grandmother ever being nine years old.

"Yes, it seemed like a good idea to me too. It was a long time ago, but I'll never forget what I picked for myself."

"What was it?" asked the boy, feeling himself being drawn into the story.

"It was a doll who had been dressed to look like Little

Bo-Peep." His grandmother paused, closing her eyes for a moment as though she was seeing the doll once again in her mind. "She had soft, brown curls, deep, blue eyes that actually opened and shut, and the longest lashes I'd ever seen."

"She sounds wonderful."

"She was," his grandmother replied softly.

"When the time came for opening presents, the first girl got a doctor's kit. There was a real stethoscope, candy pills, a thermometer that wouldn't break, and compartments for all the things to make pretending to be a doctor seem almost real."

"The next girl got a makeup kit, with a mirror and all sorts of good-smelling lotions and creams. It came in a red-flowered box with golden hinges. It was easy to imagine the fun she was going to have, pretending to be grown-up.

"But the third girl opened the very best present of all. It was roller skates. I can still remember seeing them in her box. They were soft, white leather . . . you know, the kind that smells so good. There was a great puff of light blue yarn down by each toe and a tiny bell that tinkled whenever she moved. The wheels were silver-colored. They were so brightly polished, it almost hurt to look at them. I could just imagine her skimming along the sidewalks, like a beautiful swan with white and silver feet. It was a wonderful, wonderful present, something I had never imagined." The grandmother sighed.

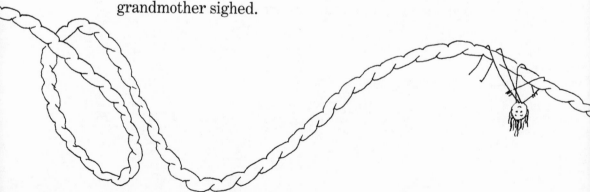

"When it was my turn, my friend gave me her box. Her face was all shining and happy, because she was giving me exactly what I had asked for. Sure enough, when I unwrapped the package the doll I had chosen was lying there. I pretended to be surprised and excited, so my friend would be pleased and the other children wouldn't guess our secret. When I got home, I put the doll on a shelf. While she was very beautiful, I never took her down. I never played with her, and I always wondered if I hadn't chosen her if I might have gotten roller skates instead."

The boy was silent for a long time. "I'm going to miss you," he said softly. The two of them walked together to the grandmother's back gate.

"I will miss you too," she said, pausing to give him one last, lingering hug. She hesitated for an instant, then smiled. "Give me your notebook. I have something for you to remember me by."

Opening the book's rings, she took some of the blank pages from the back and interspersed them throughout her grandson's itinerary.

"What are you doing?" the boy asked, taking the book back from her.

"I'm leaving you space for the most important part of your journey," she answered, looking at him tenderly. "I'm leaving you space for the unexpected."

*What if
the possibilities
we see in life
are limited
by the boundaries
of our expectations?*

## The Bird in the Barn

"I don't know how much longer I can do this," the boy thought, scrubbing away an unwanted tear and kicking a pebble halfheartedly ahead of him. "I've been sitting on the bench all season. It isn't fair. I need to practice and the coach just doesn't like me. So what if I can't hit the ball or throw it as far as the other guys? I'm the fastest runner on the team." He kicked the pebble again, sending it skittering into the tall grass at the side of the road. "Guess being fastest doesn't count for anything if I can't hit the ball. I've tried as hard as I can," he thought sadly, brushing away another tear. It was bad enough he was going to disappoint his father. He didn't want to be a baby too.

Early every morning, while the rest of the family slept,

his father took the metal lunch box his wife had packed the night before and slipped silently out the door to catch the bus to work. By the time he got back home at night, the boy had finished his homework and was nearly ready for bed. The boy loved his father as much as he hated their evening conversations. "How was baseball today?" he'd ask. "Okay." "Hit any home runs?" "Not today, Dad." "Keep trying, son, you need to keep trying." "I will, Dad, I will."

A gust of wind touched the troubled boy's face. He lifted his head and eased himself into a trot. Picking up the pace, he started to run. He ran without thinking and without realizing that he had passed the outskirts of the town. He ran until he saw a weathered, old barn just ahead of him, then slowed to catch his breath. The rusty, red pump standing off to one side reminded the boy of his thirst.

"Excuse me, sir," he said, speaking to the farmer who

seemed to have come from nowhere. "May I have some water?"

The farmer nodded. "Looks like you need to sit down and rest a spell," he drawled, motioning the boy into the coolness of the barn and offering him a seat on a fresh cut bale of hay.

"It's a nice barn, sir," the boy said.

"It'll do," the man replied simply. He wasn't much for conversation.

The boy looked in amazement at the old barn's wide plank floors and hand-pegged wooden rafters. It was like stepping back in time. The farmer followed his gaze. "Hasn't changed much, 'cept now we have 'lectricity. Yup," he said, as though he were speaking to himself, "my grandpa milked his cows in here by lantern light." The boy was quiet.

"Looks like you're running away from somethin'," the

farmer guessed, pulling a blade of hay from the bale and placing the end in his mouth.

The boy slumped down in his seat and rested his head in his hands. "I'm no good at baseball," he confessed. "My dad is going to be so disappointed. I keep trying, but I just can't do it. Guess I'll never amount to anything." He sighed.

Before the farmer had a chance to respond, the silence was broken by the sound of crashing overhead. "What's that?" asked the boy, looking up. For the first time he noticed a small cobweb-covered window lighting the corner of the loft.

"Happens all the time," the farmer replied matter-of-factly.

"What happens?" asked the boy, looking harder toward the window.

"Every summer birds come into the barn to roost. Most of 'em fly away after a spell, but a few always fly up to the loft, then try to get out that there window."

"But the window is closed," the boy said incredulously.

"Yup," answered the farmer. "I never could quite figure it out. Guess they think it's the only way out. Seems like the harder they try, the more scared they git."

"What happens then?" the boy asked.

"Mostly they try till they can't try any longer. Some of them actually kill themselves on the glass. The rest of them just quit and lie there till they die. If I'm here when it happens, I always go up to rescue 'em," he said, motioning to the tall, thin ladder leading to the loft.

"I'll do it, sir," the boy said, hurrying to the ladder.

There on the loft's dusty floor lay a frightened heap of feathers. The boy walked slowly toward the little bird, and cupping it gently in his hands, carried it down the ladder, and released it. He watched in silence as the tiny creature gradually recovered itself and flew slowly out of sight. "He tried so hard to get through that window," the boy said, shaking his head sadly. "He never even noticed this huge, wide open door."

The farmer walked out of the barn, hesitated for a moment, then laid his hand on the boy's thin shoulder. "We always have other choices, son," he said quietly. "Sometimes we just need to look beyond our fear to see them."

"Maybe I'll amount to something after all," the boy answered softly, remembering the joy he felt in running. He set off down the road, and the farmer watched until he disappeared from sight. "Yup," he said, hitching up his overalls and heading back into the barn. "Maybe he will."

*The more willingly*
*we look*
*for alternatives,*
*the less*
*we find to fear.*

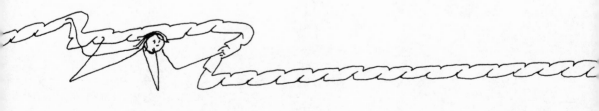

# The Storm

The call to her father would need to be brief, she thought, but their rare phone calls always were. When her mother was alive, she'd written occasional letters. Now she didn't bother. She and her father had never had much to say to each other. She remembered when she was a little girl, watching from the window as he left their small cottage, carrying the yellow rain slicker fishermen in their town always wore.

Sometimes when she thought of him, she could still see his arms: strong, sinewy, covered with hair, bleached almost colorless from a lifetime in the sun. She remembered his hands, too, scarred from years of baiting cruel hooks, hauling in nets, and fighting with the ocean for his share of her grudging bounty. While she could still almost see the broad, blunt span of his fingers, she could never remember feeling their touch.

For the first time in her life, she gathered her courage to ask him for something. She cleared her throat and took a deep breath. She couldn't give him the opportunity to say no.

"Dad, it's me. Yes, I know it's been a long time since we talked. My company wants me to go to China for a year, and I can't bring Molly. She's six now, Dad. You're her only relative. I need to leave her with you. We're flying out on Friday. I have a layover there. If you meet us at the airport, I can give her to you and still make my overseas connection. Yes, I know you never approved of me wanting to raise a child on my own. She's a wonderful little girl, Dad. I'm going to miss her so much, but I need to do this and I know she'll be safe there with you."

The fisherman looked over at the frightened little girl sitting beside him in his car. What was he going to do with the child? She was so skinny and pale. "City living," he scoffed to himself, "can't be good for anyone. Look at her, a good breeze would blow her away." He hadn't wanted to take the girl, but his daughter had given him no choice. He was used to living by himself, and he liked it that way. "No need to talk to anyone or deal with their foolish nonsense," he thought, fondly recalling the times he'd spent alone in his boat.

He was too old now to put out to sea. His eyes were no longer clear, and he'd lost both the strength and the will to do a daily battle with the wind and water. He'd established a solitary routine that he liked; even his afternoons on the bench at the beach were solitary. He didn't invite conversation. Now this girl would spoil all that. He remembered how he'd hated storms and the way they disrupted the otherwise predictable pattern of his life. "This storm is going to last a whole year," he thought angrily, looking at the unwanted child, who had shrunk as far away from him as her seat belt would allow. "At least she's not chattering."

He stopped the car abruptly. "Well, we're home now, might as well get out." He walked briskly up the walkway to his front door, not waiting for her to follow.

The unpacking didn't take long. "I'm going to the beach," he announced. "You can either come with me or stay here by yourself." Something in the child's silence told him that, while she was afraid of him, she was even more afraid of staying alone. "I'll make us both a sandwich," he said, in what he hoped was a somewhat kinder voice. "There's a bench near the water where I usually sit. Maybe you'd like to play in the sand."

She was so different from the boisterous, carefree children he knew. Still wearing her sandals, she walked cautiously along the beach, as though unaccustomed to the feel of sand between her toes. The fisherman watched as she bent to gather shiny stones and delicate shells, noticing how she took the time to appreciate each one. "Funny," he

thought, "how I never had much interest in such things."
When she came back, she was carrying a pail and shovel
some other child had left behind. It was the first time he'd
seen her smile.

She knelt quietly beside him, filling the pail with sand
and piling it into a cool, damp mound. She worked until the
mound was nearly as high as the seat of his bench, then,
hesitating as though she was attempting something entirely
new, began building a sand castle.

The fisherman noticed how diligently she worked and
how painstakingly she decorated each of the castle windows
with differing colors of seaweed and stone. He felt so
unexpectedly touched by the way she wound her seashell

road in the direction of his bench that the fishing boats he usually watched crossed the horizon unobserved.

When the castle was finished, the child's eyes shone with pleasure and pride. "Tomorrow," she told the old man, turning to speak with him for the first time, "tomorrow I'll bring my doll here to play."

"Maybe this won't be quite as bad as I imagined," he thought, watching her take off her shoes. As the two of them walked back to the cottage, he surprised himself by humming the tune from a long-forgotten song.

Late that night a storm began to brew. The grasses beyond the beach lay flat and wet beneath its chilling winds.

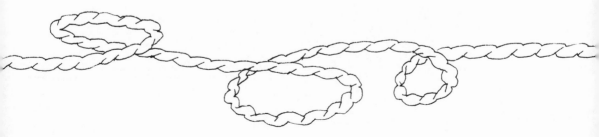

Threatening clouds replaced the stars. Bolts of lightning lit the waves as an angry ocean hurled them onto the beach. When the storm had passed, all that remained of the castle was a flattened pile of seaweed and stones.

In the morning when they returned, the old man thought he could not bear the look of sadness in his granddaughter's eyes. "Come," he said, pointing to the beach. "We'll find the treasures you need for a new castle." Heads down, the two of them began their walk.

"Look," said the girl, encouraged by his help. "The seaweed is much fresher and greener than what I used yesterday."

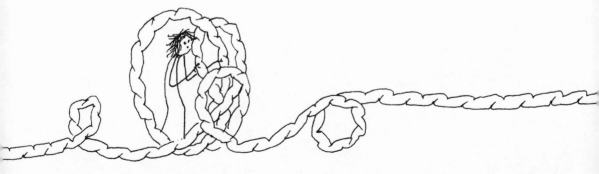

"This starfish will be perfect on the top of your castle," the old man answered, holding it out to her.

"I see a piece of red cloth I can use for a flag," she said excitedly, running ahead to pick it up.

"And here's a shell that hums the secret song of the ocean," responded the fisherman, pressing it gently against her ear.

"Grandfather," she said, using his name for the first time. "None of these beautiful things were here yesterday." She tucked her tiny hand into his as they walked together toward his bench. He held it tenderly, feeling the softness of her skin and the fragile strength of her fingers.

As he eased himself into a sitting position, the old man thought of how he had resented her coming and of the many gentle changes she'd already brought to his life, changes he'd never imagined he needed.

"There's almost never a storm," he replied thoughtfully, smoothing her hair as he spoke, "that doesn't leave something new on the beach."

*The more we view
change as
something to resist,
the less we see
and celebrate
the treasures
it holds.*

# Arranging Furniture

"Hi. What a great morning for a walk," the woman in the purple sweatsuit said, greeting her neighbor as the two reached their regular meeting place. The daily exercise was wonderful for both of them, and the fear of disappointing each other helped to keep them consistent.

"How's your daughter-in-law?" the neighbor asked, putting her hands in the pockets of her red slacks and picking up their conversation from the previous day.

"All right, I guess," her friend replied, frowning. "Somehow there always seems to be a sort of tension between us." She watched a scarlet autumn leaf drift lazily to the ground ahead of her, then continued.

"The other day I went over for a few hours to watch the children so she could go to the store. While they were napping, I straightened her linen closet; then, as I was walking past her answering machine, I noticed how many messages she had and cleared them for her. She's always so busy, I thought it would help if I listed the calls in order of their importance."

"Did your daughter-in-law appreciate your thoughtfulness?" the woman in the red sweatsuit asked.

"Not at all," the woman in purple replied. "She wasn't the least bit grateful. While it was perfectly obvious I meant well, she acted as though I was continually interfering with her life!"

"That must have made you feel awful," the woman in

the red outfit said sympathetically, suddenly remembering a similar incident from her past.

She walked silently for a few minutes, gathering together the threads of her memory, then went on. "When I was about ten," she said, "my mother had a friend who owned the most wonderful little dog. Whenever she went for a visit, I begged to come along so I could play with him. One day while we were there, her friend got an important phone call. She asked us to make ourselves comfortable for a few minutes, then carried the phone into the next room.

"My mother was a wonderful homemaker," the woman in red remembered, smiling. "She was always trying something new to make our home seem more inviting. The moment her friend left the room, she pointed to the sofa.

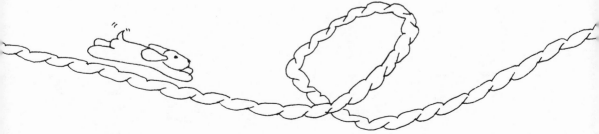

'I've always thought this would look much better under the window,' she said. 'Help me move it, dear.'"

"Did the two of you actually move the sofa?" the woman in the purple sweatsuit asked in disbelief.

"We not only moved the sofa," her friend responded, "we moved two big wing chairs as well. When we'd finished, my mother looked very pleased and stood back for a moment to enjoy her handiwork. After that, she moved a couple small tables and started arranging some of the little treasures her friend had on the mantel. It was a great improvement. I could hardly wait for the woman to come back, so I could see the look of pleasure on her face.

"My mother's friend finished her conversation just about the time my mother was rehanging a picture, pounding a nail into the wall with the heel of her shoe. . . . And the look on her face was not at all what I'd expected!"

"I'd have been horrified," the woman in the purple sweatsuit said. "I suppose your mother meant well, but arranging someone's furniture without asking permission was a terribly disrespectful thing to do."

"It probably was," her friend answered, nodding, "but at the time, it just felt as though we were being helpful."

The woman in the purple sweatsuit was suddenly silent. "Do you suppose," she asked slowly, "that meaning well just isn't enough? What if arranging someone's furniture without permission is no more disrespectful than doing the same thing with even the smallest part of their life?"

"I never thought about it before," the woman in red replied. "But I suppose it's time I did. I don't know about you," she continued, laughing just a little uncomfortably, "but I certainly don't want 'She Meant Well' on my tombstone!"

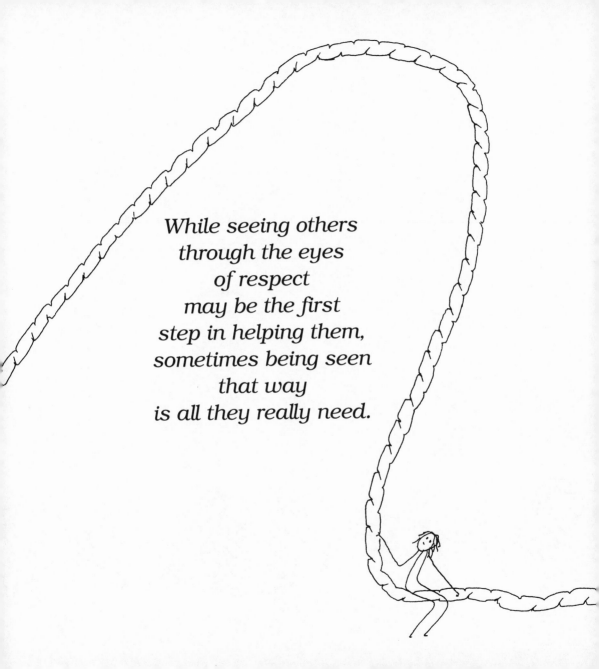

*While seeing others*
*through the eyes*
*of respect*
*may be the first*
*step in helping them,*
*sometimes being seen*
*that way*
*is all they really need.*

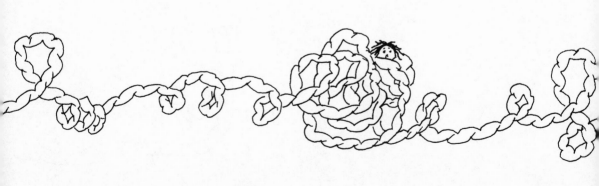

# From Where We Stand

The couple who stood pressed against the small ship's rail was no longer young. She leaned against the bulk of him, looking for a moment at the broad, sure hand that held her close. "Both of us had other lives, other husbands, other wives." She smiled briefly at the rhyme she'd unintentionally created. While she had neither the will nor the desire to be married again, she had told him he was her last love, and she meant it. Now here they were, the two of them, in the place that advertised itself as the honeymoon capital of the world. She smiled again.

The *Maid of the Mist* made her regular, unrelenting voyage at the base of Niagara Falls. The woman shuddered.

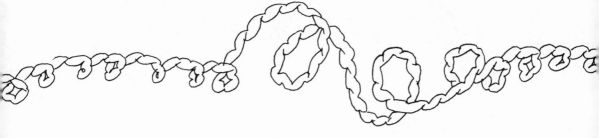

While she knew she was safe, the enormous power of the water frightened her. "This is terrifying," she shouted, trying to make her voice heard above the crashing of the waves. "I can't wait for the ride to be over." He drew her closer, as she knew he would. She leaned against him, willing herself to focus on the rainbow and wondering how many of their yellow-clad fellow travelers felt as frightened and overwhelmed as she.

"There's an observation tower with a rotating restaurant on the other side," he said, pointing as they disembarked. "It might be fun to eat dinner there and see the falls at night." She nodded, appreciating his thoughtfulness.

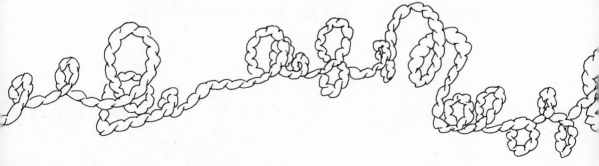

Now it was the end of the day, and there were just two seats remaining by the window. "This is perfect," the man said, gazing across the table and feeling the sort of tenderness that often touched him when he looked at her.

He'd have done anything to take care of her, but it wasn't easy. While she was the most loving woman he had ever known, she was also stubbornly independent and annoyingly self-contained. He watched as a look of delight swept across her face. "Look," she said, "they've turned on the lights. See how beautiful the falls are. They look so magnificent and magical from here." He nodded, reaching for her hand across the table and feeling relieved that she seemed to have forgotten her fear.

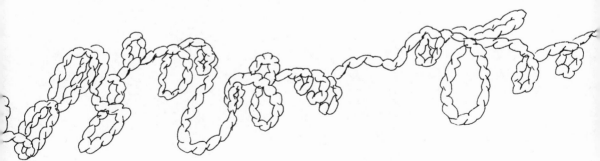

"When I was younger," he told her, "I had a summer job on a lake in Vermont. I had never been in New England before and was especially fascinated by the quaint little town nearby."

The woman smiled. "This dear man is such a wonderful storyteller," she thought to herself. She reached for her wine and leaned forward.

"On my days off," he continued, "I used rolls and rolls of film, taking pictures of each building. I photographed doorways and windows, walkways and gardens. Somehow I felt the need to carry each detail away with me when the summer was ended.

"On my last weekend in Vermont, a friend invited me to

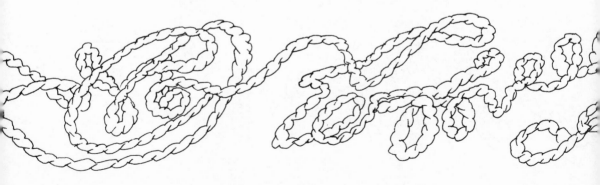

climb the small precipice that rose above the town. The
higher we climbed, the more my perspective changed. In the
beginning, some of the details simply started to fade, then
the most interesting thing happened. I began to see how the
gardens and walkways connected the buildings and drew
them together into a village. The individual people suddenly
seemed to be connected too. I'd been seeing them all summer
without ever noticing how they formed a community."

"Do you think that means that the farther we get away
from something, the more clearly we see it?" she asked,
thinking of the falls and how beautiful they looked from a
distance.

"I suppose sometimes that's true," he replied, thinking

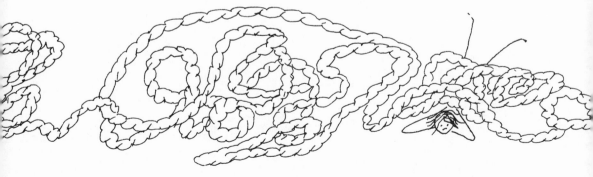

about his answer before he spoke. "Mostly, I guess, what we see depends on where we're standing when we look.

"From where you stand does marriage still seem out of the question?" he teased, knowing the answer before he spoke.

"Good try," she said, smiling. "From where I stand, you are and will always be my last and dearest love."

He took her hand and pressed her fingers to his lips. "The world is a different place," he thought, "and from where I stand, this is good enough for me."

*What we see
as we look at our world
usually depends
on our vantage point.*

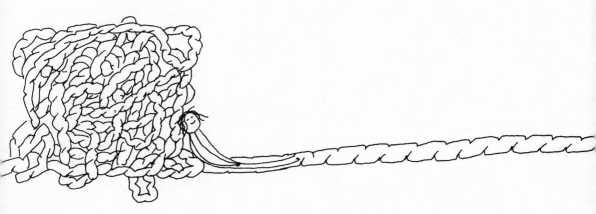

# Other Kinds of Angels

"My father is so sick," he said, trying to speak matter-of-factly and shifting the dish towel in his hand. "This will probably be his last Christmas."

"I know," his wife responded softly. She had never ceased to feel amazed by the differences between them. The only times he helped with the things he called women's work were when he needed to talk.

"Let's try to make this a perfect Christmas," she said, rinsing a dinner plate and placing it in the rack. She sighed, thinking of their lives together and how far they had strayed from her dream of perfection. "Maybe this Christmas can change all that," she thought wistfully, hardly able to hope for the possibility of such a miracle.

"We could start with the tree," she said, wiping the kitchen counter and putting the last pot away.

"What's wrong with the one we have now?" he growled warily. "We've been using it for years."

"That's just it," she said, grimacing. "It's fake. It looks like a huge green toilet brush."

"I like it," he said.

"This year, it needs to be real," she answered emphatically, imagining the fragrant smell of fresh-cut pine.

After her husband left the kitchen, the woman settled herself in a chair, bringing with her the box of yellowing holiday magazines she'd been saving for so long. How could

she make this Christmas perfect, she wondered, when everything around them was so lacking in perfection? She looked at the faded wallpaper and the scratches of living on the table by her chair.

What ever happened to all those dreams of the perfect family that had lived in her imagination for so long? Shaking her head, she tried to remember the last time the four of them had enjoyed a peaceful evening around the fire. "All of us just get so busy," she thought, staring wistfully at a candlelit living room in the magazine picture. "This is how I always wanted our lives to look."

She took extra time with the Christmas cards and spent hours shopping for the perfect presents, wrapping each of them with care. The delicious cookies and sweets she so carefully baked disappeared long before she could arrange them artistically, forcing her to spend more time in the kitchen than she had planned.

December arrived without any snow. Disappointed yet still hopeful, the woman continued to shop, bake, clean, decorate, and plan. Everything should have been perfect, but it wasn't. Her preparations left her feeling tired and unappreciated. The latest batch of Christmas cookies burned, there were still more cards to send, and the needles were already falling from the tree.

By the time the day arrived, the perfect Christmas

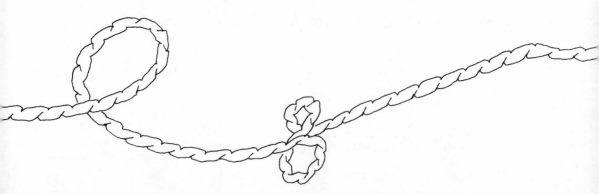

she'd worked so hard to create seemed to be everywhere but in her home. Feeling heartsick and disappointed, she watched quietly as her family unwrapped their gifts, then reached out somewhat forlornly to receive one of her own.

Untying the bow slowly, she glanced at the card, then stared in disbelief at the contents of the box. Her younger sister had made what she said was a kitchen angel, but the creature lying amidst the tissue bore absolutely no resemblance to the woman's blond-haired, nymph-bodied, white-clad mental image of the way a perfect angel should look.

She was about ten inches long and made of papier-

mâché, with short brown hair fashioned from wads of typing paper dipped in coffee-colored paste. Her arms and legs ended with such abruptness that harp playing and golden stair climbing were entirely out of the question. Her body, which was totally naked except for two rather undistinguished wings, was decidedly more lumpy than cherubic and immodestly sported a pair of flaccid and sadly misshapen breasts.

"My whole life looks like this pathetic little angel," the woman thought sadly, lifting the awkward creature from its wrappings and pausing to finish her sister's note. "Merry

Christmas," it read. "This imperfect angel comes to remind you that the most perfect part of living is love."

The woman's eyes suddenly filled with tears of genuine gratitude as she felt the truth of her sister's words. "I've spent far too much of my life," she thought remorsefully, "looking through my eyes and not my heart."

Glancing at her family, she saw her mother-in-law reach out to touch her sick husband's frail hand. Their predictably aloof teenage son had quietly draped his lanky body on the arm of his sister's chair, and for a brief moment she was certain she'd seen tears of appreciation sparkle in her husband's eyes. Looking out the window, she noticed huge, soft, white snowflakes beginning to fall. Inside, the love she felt around her seemed strong enough to touch.

"It's amazing how much perfection there is in life," she thought, looking back at the present in her lap, "when we start noticing other kinds of angels."

*When we look*
*at life*
*through the eyes*
*of our heart,*
*the perfection that*
*already exists*
*is easier to see.*

# Stale Peanuts

The days of the cherished "week all alone" were passing much too fast. "What will you do without us?" they had asked, when they discovered that the children's school field trip coincided with her husband's West Coast convention. "My precious burdens," she thought tenderly, understanding their inability to see her as anything but an extension of themselves. "I'll be fine," she reassured them. "I'll probably drive up to the lake and close the cottage for the winter."

She hadn't told her family about the pictures she longed to paint, and how she dreamed of becoming an artist. She didn't want them to know how much she secretly blamed them for keeping her too busy. Now she was about to have seven glorious days without interruption. It was almost too much to imagine.

At first the cottage felt empty. She lit the faithful old wood-burning cook stove and waited, still wearing her jacket, until the comfort and warmth of its fire slowly filled the kitchen. She told herself there was plenty of time. "I should bring in some wood before I start painting," she thought, "and the groceries need to be put away." By the time she'd finished the rest of her self-appointed tasks, dusk had fallen and the watercolor paper remained untouched. Feeling anxious, she poured a cup of tea, carried her paint and brushes to the kitchen table and arranged them in an orderly fashion.

She knew the scene she wanted to create. It lived so clearly in her mind, she could almost feel the warmth of its sunlight and the coolness of its shadows. "What if I can't do this?" she thought, feeling the finger of fear touch her heart. The fear wasn't new, it had lived inside her ever since she had begun to think of painting. She looked down at bleak whiteness of the paper and a feeling of nausea wrapped itself around her so tightly, she could barely breathe. "Maybe I just need a good night's sleep," she thought. Turning off the light, she headed wearily to bed.

Almost as soon as she closed her eyes, an elderly woman appeared in her dreams. The woman fastened her thinning white hair with a simple silver comb, pulled a faded turquoise gown from an old trunk and slipped it silently over her head. Standing in front of the mirror for a moment, she smiled approvingly at her reflection, then, feeling happy and expectant, set out for a long-awaited celebration.

The ballroom was even more beautiful than the woman

in the dream had imagined. As the orchestra played her favorite waltz, huge baskets of flowers filled the air with their fragrance. Across the room she could see a table heavily laden with an assortment of delicious food. Suddenly realizing how hungry she was, she took a few steps forward, then stopped abruptly just outside the door. The ballroom looked so large and crowded. "What if I'm not dressed appropriately?" she wondered.

Seeing a large bowl of peanuts, she put a handful in her mouth. Noticing their flat and unappealing taste, she wrinkled her nose. "They're stale," she thought. "Well, at least they're nutritious." She looked out at the ballroom and took a few more peanuts. "What if I trip and fall when I'm walking across the floor?" Feeling sickened by the thought, the old woman reached again for the nuts. "I'm the only one who's come alone," she thought, wondering if the people there saw her as a poor, pathetic person in a faded turquoise dress. "I can't walk across that room by myself; besides, the peanuts have satisfied me. I'm not hungry anymore."

Taking one last look at the feast, the elderly woman left the celebration. Safely back home, she unfastened the silver barrette, laid her dress in the trunk, and slipped quietly back out of the dream.

"All she had was stale peanuts," the woman thought, awaking with a feeling of emptiness inside. "She never even tasted the feast! She was so afraid to walk across the ballroom, she kept focusing on the reasons she couldn't try." She sat upright in the bed. While the room was still dark, she suddenly saw very clearly.

"I've been so afraid I really can't paint, I've been blaming my family and my daily tasks for keeping me from trying. I want so much more than stale peanuts in my life," she thought emphatically, "and the only one who keeps me from that dream is me."

Pulling on her robe, she walked barefoot across the cold linoleum kitchen floor to relight the old wood-burning stove. "The feast is waiting," she thought, dipping a brush in water and touching its tip to the paint. "I wonder if a butterfly feels as frightened as I just before it leaves its cocoon?"

When we find
ourselves
blaming
others
for our hunger,
we need to look
more closely at our fear.

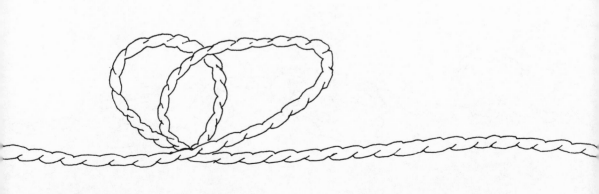

# Raindrops

"I still think you might have been switched at birth," the woman teased, looking up from the flowers in which she knelt to smile at her daughter. It was a long-standing joke between them. "How could you really be my child when you have no affinity for gardening?" The two of them laughed, and the daughter settled herself on the soft spring grass beside her mother.

"Sometimes it hurts me so," the younger woman said, looking toward the house, "when I think of that precious baby sleeping so peacefully inside. She has so many painful experiences ahead of her in life."

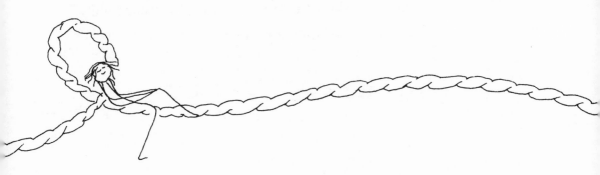

The older woman shook her head, then moved toward a stubborn weed, bending to loosen its root. While she knew her daughter didn't expect an answer, she still felt the familiar tug of tenderness that often touched her heart when they were together.

"I used to tell you that painful experiences teach us to be more compassionate and strong." Her daughter nodded. "Even though I believed it was so," her mother continued, "I'd still have done anything in my power to protect you."

"I know, Mom," the younger woman answered softly. "Sometimes even now, when things seem especially hard, I can still hear you asking me, 'What can you learn from this?'"

"I suppose we do the best we can in raising our family," her mother replied, wrapping a support around the newly budded peony bush. "Hopefully we learn from our mistakes and our children find a way to forgive us, but lately I've been wondering if I might have missed something along the way."

"You've been a wonderful mother," her daughter said, wanting to reassure her, "and a wonderful gardener too. Look at this perennial bed. It seems to grow more beautiful every year."

Her mother smiled. "It still needs tending, dear, but it isn't as difficult as it used to be. The more the flowers spread, the less room there seems to be for weeds."

The two of them sat quietly, enjoying both the day and each other's company. "I've been thinking about my grandmother," the older woman said, breaking the silence and gazing off into the distance for a moment. "She was so poor most of her life that she taught herself never to waste anything. She used old clothes to make quilts, bones to make soup, and sour milk to make the most delicious cookies I'd ever tasted.

"Mostly, though, I remember how she saved raindrops. She put a barrel under the gutter and collected water for us to wash our hair. She said it was nature's best conditioner. I don't remember. I only remember how cold it was and that she said we must never waste the rain.

"I know the painful times get our attention," she continued, looking at her daughter, "but lately I've been wondering if hardship is the only way to learn.

"What if joy is like the rain? What if it falls on us so gently that we take it for granted or ignore it altogether? What if we taught ourselves not to waste it, just as my grandmother learned not to waste the raindrops? Maybe it would spread like these flowers until it eventually crowded out some of the hardship and pain."

She cut a deep purple iris and handed it to her daughter. "While I often asked you what you could learn when things went wrong," she said, shaking her head somewhat sadly, "I don't remember ever asking you what you could learn from something as perfect and as beautiful as this."

The daughter looked silently at the orchidlike flower in her hand. "I think I hear the baby," she said, smiling as she rose slowly from the grass. "Thank you, Mom. It feels so wonderful to think of teaching her to learn from joy."

Her mother smiled back, feeling the familiar tug of tenderness again. "In order to teach anything, dear," she said gently, "we first need to learn it for ourselves."

*What if the lessons*
*to be learned*
*from joy*
*have been there*
*all along,*
*simply waiting for us*
*to see*
*and use them?*

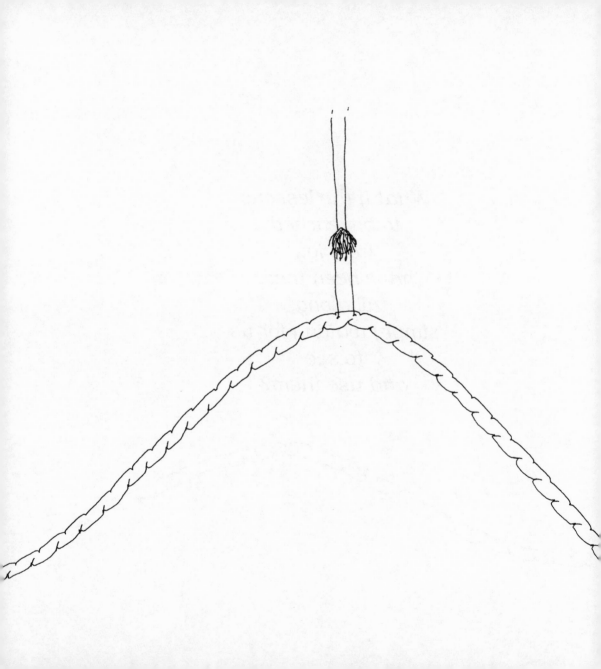

# The Path

The lanky, dark-haired, fortyish man stared unseeing at his reflection in the mirror and straightened the knot in his tie. Waving to the children, he blew his wife a perfunctory kiss, then took the cup of coffee she held out to him. With the habitual motion of a sleepwalker, he stepped into his car, started the engine, and backed carefully out the driveway. It was going to be another grueling day.

Thinking of his family, he grimaced at his ever-present sense of guilt. While he loved them, this was the time of his life when he needed to focus on climbing the corporate ladder. Tightening his grip on the steering wheel, he glanced into the rearview mirror, then guided his car onto the expressway.

As he merged into the endless flow of city-bound vehicles, his mind drifted back in time, to the old farm in New England where he and his parents had spent their summers. He smiled, remembering how instantly they'd fallen in love with the place.

Almost automatically the man turned on his blinker and changed lanes. "Early in our exploration," he recalled, returning to his musings, "we found an abandoned family cemetery, not far from the house. The trees and underbrush had grown up around it so tightly, the ancient stone markers were almost impossible to see.

"We wanted to honor the memory of the people who had

built our barn and worked our fields," the man remembered, thinking of that day so many years ago. "My father set to work gathering tools to clear a path, but my mother just stood quietly, staring at the task that lay ahead. I remember how she smiled," he thought, "then she took off that long green scarf she always wore and tied it to a tree beside the cemetery wall. She wanted us to be able to see what we were working toward.

"It is amazing how clear the memory still is," the man thought, applying his brakes automatically and glancing at the sprawl of buildings that surrounded the highway. "We spent days clearing away underbrush, pulling up thorn-

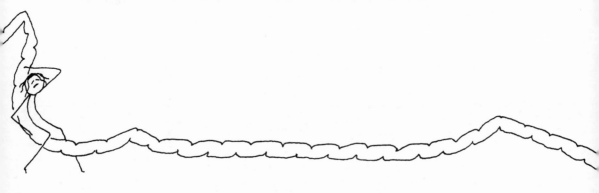

covered vines, and cutting down the trees that stood in our way. It was backbreaking labor for uncallused city folks. We were cut and scratched and exhausted by the time we finished, but it was such a triumphant feeling to walk back to the farmhouse on the path we had cleared for ourselves!"

The man smiled and eased into the right lane, anticipating his exit. "That night, when we told one of the old farmers about our adventure," he remembered, "he got the strangest look on his face, then told us that most of the original cemeteries had been built beside roads." The man guided his car expertly onto the busy city street, returning in his mind to that day so long ago. "Right after breakfast the next morning, we went back to the cemetery, walking the path we'd worked so hard to clear. Sure enough, only a short distance beyond was the old main country road."

The man slowed his car as though to absorb the importance of his memory. "There was clearly more than one way to get where we wanted to go," he thought, holding the words for a moment in his mind, "but we never used the main road. It always made us happier to follow the path we had cleared for ourselves."

He drove his car into the parking lot and sat quietly, without moving to open the door. "Living life as though I'm on a perpetual expressway isn't making me happy," he said to himself. "I wonder if what's at the top of that corporate ladder is really worth the climb?" As he thought again of his mother and of the day they began clearing their path, he felt the tension slip slowly from his body.

Mentally untying a green scarf from the top of the corporate ladder, he wrapped it tenderly around his family, then stepped slowly from the car. "I think I've just taken the first step toward clearing a path of my own," he thought. Then he noticed he was smiling.

*When we look
toward what is
truly
important in our life,
clearing
our own path
becomes much easier.*

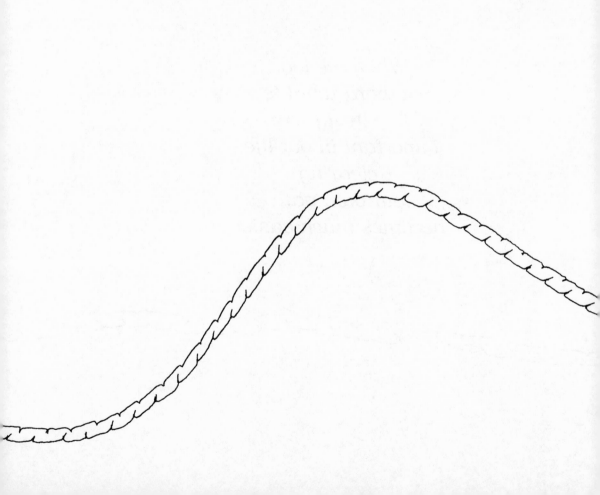

# The Backstitch

The two longtime friends climbed up onto the rocks a short distance from the beach, enjoying the view of the ocean. They spread out the old quilt they'd brought with them and leaned against the ledge that nature had provided as a backrest.

"Here," the taller woman said, opening a thermos of iced tea and pouring a drink for her friend. "It feels so wonderful to be with you. It's been years since we've done anything like this." The silence between them felt familiar and comfortable.

"Do you remember when we were pregnant together?" the shorter woman asked. They both laughed. "We must have been quite a sight, cramming ourselves into that little car of yours along with a month's supply of groceries."

"You taught me to save money by shopping with coupons and drinking powdered milk." The taller woman wrinkled her nose at the memory.

"And you taught me to make soup," her friend replied. "I still can't throw out a chicken bone without cooking it first for the broth. Do you remember how we nearly burned down the house making candles?"

"And what about all those loaves of bread we used to make? We were poor in those days, but your friendship made my life so rich, I scarcely noticed."

"I remember the day we met. It was right after Christmas, I was taking down the decorations, and you were selling cosmetics door to door. I almost didn't let you in. When I did, we started talking right away . . . about the kinds of things that really mattered. It made me realize how terribly lonely I'd been. I rushed to the kitchen the moment you left so I could bake you some cookies. I wanted to give you something so you'd like me."

"You didn't need to give me something in return for liking you. I liked you already."

"Your friendship taught me a lot about trying to get people to like me. I'm better about it than I used to be, but sometimes I feel angry at myself when I notice how important it still seems."

The two fell silent for a moment, caught up in the motion of the waves and the warmth of their memories.

"Do you ever feel like a failure in the school of life?" The taller woman sighed as she watched how effortlessly the gulls rode the air currents. "Just when I think I've given up trying to get people to like me, I notice myself doing it again. No matter how often I remind myself that moments are the most important part of life, I still catch myself running past them without paying attention, and every time I think I've learned something about letting go of guilt, it seems to creep up and hook me again. It's as though I keep needing to learn the same thing over and over. I hate it!"

"Sometimes, when I disappoint myself like that, I wonder if maybe life is like the day I learned to sew," her friend replied, reaching for the memory in her mind.

"When I was in Girl Scouts, the leader of our troop cut out a pile of yellow-and-white gingham squares and put them on the table in front of us. It was hot that day. I can still remember how damp and sticky the needle and thread felt in my hand. She began by teaching us a running stitch. When we had learned to do it well enough, she brushed back a lock of hair that had fallen across her face and leaned forward as though she was about to tell us an important secret. 'Now girls,' she said, 'this is the way to make your sewing really strong. You take two stitches forward, then one stitch back."

As we begin
to see learning
as a process
rather than a goal,
we become
more accepting and gentle
with ourselves.

# Public Bathrooms

It was nearly noon on a sunny day in mid-August, and the girl who sat in the backseat of the car was about to turn thirteen. She watched the endless fields of corn spread out on either side of the highway with a kind of curious interest that made her smile at herself. "No one would know I've been seeing them all my life," she thought. Sighing contentedly, she settled back against the cushion. Somehow everything about the day seemed fresh and new and incredibly wonderful.

Looking at the two familiar heads whose bodies were hidden from view by the back of front seat, she imagined her

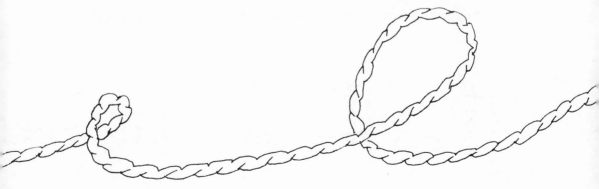

mother's hand resting gently on her father's knee. She'd seen them drive that way for longer than she could remember. The many tender ways they'd found to express their affection had made her childhood feel both happy and secure.

She'd been waiting for this time with just the two of them ever since they'd taken the same trip the year before. Life as the oldest of five children was hectic and responsible at best. The opportunity to be an only child for a few days felt almost as magical as Christmas. Only one thing marred her joy, and she willed herself not to think about it.

Her father slowed the car and slipped easily into a parking space beside the restaurant. Eating out was a special treat. "Large families can't afford to do this often," he had said, teaching her to be respectful by choosing from the least expensive entrées. She glanced at her mother and moved closer to her in the booth, as though to make herself feel better. "Maybe it won't happen this time," she hoped, dreading the moment she knew was drawing near.

When their meal was finished, her father wiped his mouth with the crisp white napkin and laid it ceremoniously beside his plate. "Why don't you two ladies use the rest room," he said courteously, "while I take care of our bill?" The girl bit her lip, then followed her mother across the restaurant.

The public rest room was tiled in pink, with blue and yellow flowers growing from the paper on its walls. While the metal partition between the stalls allowed both of them their privacy, the girl could still see her mother's feet planted

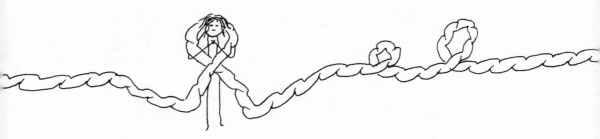

squarely in the center of her cubicle. Drawing in her breath, she watched as the woman's familiar hand moved unerringly across the floor; gathering up the bits of toilet paper those before her had carelessly let fall.

While the girl watched in undisguised horror, her mother opened the cubicle door, took one last approving look at the tidy area she'd left behind, then flushed the unwanted paper down the toilet.

Turning, she walked directly to the sink, where she gathered other people's used paper towels from the counter and deposited them unceremoniously in a nearby wastebasket.

The girl had watched the same procedure countless horrifying times before and knew in her heart that pretending not to know this woman would be to no avail. Somewhere between the toilet flushing and sink wiping, her mother always managed to smile at her or speak her name, clearly proving to everyone in the room that they were related.

The humiliation nearly complete, she rolled her eyes as her mother washed and dried her hands, then wiped the sink and counter with her own damp paper towel. "Why do you always do all that?" the girl hissed when the two of them were alone.

Pushing open the bathroom door, the woman put her arm around her daughter and drew her closer. "We need to leave things better than we found them," she said simply.

"I'm never going to embarrass my children by cleaning public bathrooms." her daughter replied in disgust.

"Perhaps not, dear," her mother answered gently, "but this may help you to remember that even the lowliest task has value, and someday, when the time is right, you'll find the way that's right for you."

*Imagine how different
the world would look
if each of us
found a simple way
to leave things
better than we found them.*

# The Writer and the Artist

*Gail Van Kleeck and Lesley Avery Gould are sisters.*
*They are the oldest and youngest daughters in a family of*
*five children who were taught that an important part of*
*living is making a difference in the world.*

*Gail Van Kleeck is a teacher and interior designer who specializes in relationship design. While raising her family she studied with Elisabeth Kübler-Ross and was active with the hospice in her area. She has carried the dream of publishing a book that might touch the lives of others for more than twenty years.*

*Lesley Avery Gould, who was once a successful New York art director, is now a videographer and teacher of the underwater world. She uses her background to create educational videos that focus on respecting our planet and ourselves.*

*Stephen Covey says, "Our greatest power is the power to change the way we see." While Gail and Lesley agree, they believe the simple lessons found in the often overlooked, ordinary moments of life sometimes hold the most powerful possibility for change.*

*By guiding their readers on this gentle journey, the sisters hope to inspire them to seek and recognize life's lessons within the texture of their own lives.*

*Dear Reader:*

*Since Lesley and I are planning to collaborate on other volumes of* How You See Anything Is How You See Everything, *we'd like to know how this book has touched your life. We would also enjoy hearing about your own experiences and how they changed something in the way you see.*

*Changing the way we see is often the first step toward both healing and a true sense of choice. It is possible that by weaving your insights into our future stories, together we can become a part of a gentler, more possibility-filled world.*

*Lesley and I look forward to hearing both your comments and experiences, and wish each of you a full and joyful life.*

*Blessings,*

*Gail Van Kleeck*

*You can contact us at 23 Highview St, Westwood, MA 02090 or on our Web site at www.simplewisdom.com.*

*Notes*

*Notes*

*Notes*

*Notes*

*Notes*

*Notes*

# Notes

*Small enough to sit on a bedside table,*
*large enough to change a life.*